HUMAN SPACEFLIGHT

ADAM FURGANG

Britannica®
Educational Publishing

IN ASSOCIATION WITH

ROSEN
EDUCATIONAL SERVICES

Published in 2018 by Britannica Educational Publishing (a trademark of Encyclopædia Britannica Inc.) in association with The Rosen Publishing Group, Inc., 29 East 21st Street, New York, NY 100

Distributed exclusively by Rosen Publishing. To see additional Britannica Educational Publishing titles, go to rosenpublishing.com.

First Edition

Britannica Educational Publishing
J.E. Luebering: Executive Director, Core Editorial
Andrea R. Field: Managing Editor, Compton's by Britannica

Rosen Publishing
Kathy Kuhtz Campbell: Senior Editor
Nelson Sá: Art Director
Brian Garvey: Series Designer/Book Layout
Cindy Reiman: Photography Manager
Karen Huang: Photo Researcher

Library of Congress Cataloging-in-Publication Data
Names: Furgang, Adam, author.
Title: Human spaceflight/Adam Furgang.
Description: First edition. | New York, NY: Britannica Educational Publishing in association with The Rosen Publishing Group, Inc., 2018. | Series: From Earth to the stars | Audience: 5–8.
Identifiers: LCCN 2016056464 | ISBN 9781680486711 (library bound) | ISBN 9781680486698 (paper book) | ISBN 9781680486704 (6 pack)
Subjects: LCSH: Manned space flight—History—Juvenile literature. | Astronauts—History—Juvenile literature. | Outer space—Exploration—Juvenile literature.
Classification: LCC TL793 .F84 2018 | DDC 629.45—dc23
LC record available at https://lccn.loc.gov/2016056464

Manufactured in the United States of America

Photo credits: Cover, p. 1 ESA/Getty Images; cover and back cover (background) nienora/Shutterstock.com; p. 5 Harold M. Lambert/Archive Photos/Getty Images; p. 7 AFP/Getty Images; pp. 9, 10–11, 20–21, 25, 32, 34, 38–39 NASA; p. 14 Encyclopædia Britannica, Inc.; pp. 16–17 Gianni Woods/NASA; pp. 18–19 JSC/NASA: p. 24 Sovfoto/Universal Images Group/Getty Images; p. 27 © AP Images; p. 31 Bill Ingalls/NASA/Getty Images; p. 33 Mark Ralston/AFP/Getty Images; p. NASA/MSFC; p. 41 NASA/JPL-Caltech/MSSS; cover banner Titima Ongkantong/Shutterstock.com; interior pages graphi pp. 8, 23, 30, 36 Hallowedland/Shutterstock.com.

CONTENTS

H ave you ever wondered what it might be like to become an astronaut, leave Earth on a rocket, and visit outer space? If so, you are not alone. Throughout history, humanity has always looked to the sky and dreamed of exploring the realm beyond Earth.

In 2000, scientists discovered evidence that even early humans looked toward the stars with wonder when some paintings on the walls of the famous caves in Lascaux, France, were uncovered. Depicted on a cave wall was a representation of a three-pointed constellation of stars, known today as the Summer Triangle. The cave paintings are thought to be more than 16,000 years old.

Though outer space continues to hold many mysteries, our knowledge of the solar system has made great leaps since the mid-twentieth century. The space age—as this period of exploration has been called—began with an unmanned flight. On October 4, 1957, the Soviet Union became the first nation to send a man-made satellite, *Sputnik 1*, into orbit around Earth. This historic achievement urged the United States to accelerate its space program. On July 29, 1958, US president Dwight D. Eisenhower signed the National Aeronautics and Space Act, creating the National Aeronautics and Space Administration (NASA). This federal agency continues to coordinate the country's space program today.

The era of human spaceflight began on April 12, 1961, when the Soviet Union launched cosmonaut Yury Gagarin into space. Gagarin orbited Earth once aboard the

On May 5, 1961, US astronaut Alan Shepard became the first American to travel in space when he made a fifteen-minute suborbital flight in the *Freedom 7* spacecraft.

Vostok 1 spacecraft. The United States followed less than a month later by sending military test pilot Alan Shepard into space on May 5, 1961. The competition between the United States and the Soviet Union for the greatest achievements in spaceflight during the twentieth century became known as the "space race." In 1963, Valentina Tereshkova became the first woman in space. It was not until 1983 that the United States launched its first female astronaut, Sally Ride, into space.

On May 25, 1961, US president John F. Kennedy issued a bold challenge to NASA, saying, "I believe that this nation should commit itself to achieving the goal, before this decade is out, of landing a man on the moon and returning him safely to Earth." NASA lived up to the challenge with the Apollo program, and on July 20, 1969, the United States landed the first manned mission on the moon. Astronaut Neil Armstrong became the first person to set foot on the moon. After taking his first step onto the lunar surface, he said, "That's one small step for [a] man, one giant leap for mankind."

The space race continued for many years. The United States achieved five more manned moon landings along with many other unmanned missions. Despite their rivalry, the Americans and Soviets eventually began working together on space missions in 1975 with the Apollo-Soyuz Test Project.

During the 1970s, the United States developed a new space vehicle, the space shuttle. The space shuttle was a rocket-propelled spacecraft that could land safely on a runway on its return, similar to a plane, and be reused for future missions. The first shuttle lifted off into space on April 12,

The space shuttle *Columbia* descends to a runway at Edwards Air Force Base in California on April 14, 1981, marking the conclusion of the first space shuttle mission (STS-1).

1981. In 2011, after more than 130 missions, the shuttle *Atlantis* made the program's final flight.

After the retirement of the shuttle, the United States concentrated its efforts on developing a new rocket and vehicle to carry humans farther into space than they have ever traveled before. Meanwhile, Russian spacecraft continued to ferry astronauts to the International Space Station, while China began a manned spaceflight program of its own. With NASA's planned mission to Mars in sight, the future of human spaceflight is more exciting than ever before.

CHAPTER 1

THE US SPACE PROGRAM

During the space race with the Soviet Union and afterward, the United States had several different space programs, each with varied goals and objectives. With each of the programs, scientists gained new insights about the effects of space travel on humans. Each program built on the knowledge gained before it, and greater goals were achieved over time.

PROJECT MERCURY

Project Mercury was the first US program to put humans in space. It began in 1958 as a response to Soviet efforts in space travel. According to NASA, the program's goals were "to orbit a manned spacecraft around Earth, to investigate man's ability to function in space," and "to recover both man and spacecraft safely."

After the selection and training of seven military test pilots, NASA had its astronauts for the Mercury program. NASA introduced the men on April 9, 1959. The astronauts—Scott Carpenter, Gordon Cooper, John Glenn, Gus Grissom,

Mercury spacecraft *Friendship 7*, carrying astronaut John Glenn, launches in 1962. Riding into space in a capsule that sat atop a modified Atlas missile, Glenn became the first American to orbit Earth.

Wally Schirra, Alan Shepard, and Deke Slayton—became known as the Mercury Seven.

Every flight of the Mercury project used a small space capsule designed to sit atop a launch rocket. The capsules were so small that they could hold only one astronaut, and there was so little room that the passenger could not even get up to move around. Project Mercury sent a total of six flights into space, with a different astronaut each time. Shepard made the first flight on May 5, 1961. The only one of the Mercury Seven not to make his own flight was Deke Slayton, who could not fly because of a heart condition that was discovered after he was chosen for the project. He eventually flew as an astronaut aboard the joint US-Soviet Apollo-Soyuz Test Project in 1975.

Two of the six Mercury launches achieved suborbital flight. The four remaining flights achieved full orbit and circled Earth before coming down. Project Mercury was completed in 1963.

PROJECT GEMINI

Before Project Mercury ended, NASA announced the second manned space program, Project Gemini. The project included ten manned missions, the first on March 23, 1965. The Gemini program

On June 3, 1965, *Gemini 4* astronaut Edward White became the first American to walk in space. During a twenty-three-minute walk, he was tethered to the spacecraft and held a device to help him move around.

helped get NASA ready to meet President Kennedy's challenge of achieving a moon landing before the end of the 1960s. The name "Gemini" refers to the twin stars Castor and Pollux in the constellation Gemini and was chosen because the new space capsules held a two-person crew.

According to NASA, the project's goals were "to subject man and equipment to spaceflight up to two weeks in duration, to rendezvous and dock with orbiting vehicles and to maneuver the docked combination by using the target vehicle's propulsion system," and "to perfect methods of entering the atmosphere and landing at a preselected point on land."

This ambitious project required new technologies. These inventions included a modified, two-stage Titan II rocket, which was originally used as a missile.

The project met most of its goals, eventually achieving an orbit around Earth lasting two weeks. One of the spacecraft also connected with another spacecraft for the first time, which would allow for longer and more complex space travel in the future, including the delivery of supplies and astronauts to a vehicle already in space. The only project goal that was not met was a ground landing, which was called off in 1964. Project Gemini was completed in 1966.

PROJECT APOLLO

Landing astronauts on the moon and returning them safely to Earth was NASA's prime goal for the 1960s. This project, called Apollo, began in 1961 and continued alongside Project Mercury and Project Gemini.

The Apollo program also had aims beyond a moon landing. According to NASA, the program's goals were "establishing the technology to meet other national interests in space, achieving preeminence in space for the United States, carrying out a program of scientific exploration of the Moon," and "developing man's capability to work in the lunar environment."

The spacecraft that NASA designed for the Apollo missions included connected Command and Service Modules, with room for three astronauts. Another component, the Lunar Module, was designed to detach from the spacecraft to land two astronauts on the moon and bring them back to the lunar orbiting Apollo craft.

The first manned Apollo flight was delayed by a tragic accident. A fire broke out in the *Apollo 1* spacecraft during a ground rehearsal on January 27, 1967, killing all three astronauts. After months of investigation and redesign, Project Apollo continued.

The first of eleven manned Apollo flights took place in October 1968. The first four flights tested the spacecraft in Earth and lunar orbit. The first mission to achieve a moon landing was *Apollo 11*, in July 1969. Neil A. Armstrong and Edwin E. Aldrin Jr. walked on the moon as the third astronaut, Michael Collins, remained in the Command and Service Module. Armstrong and Aldrin collected rocks to bring back to Earth, conducted research, and studied the surrounding area. The Lunar Module then brought them back to the Command and Service Module for their return

Apollo Command Module

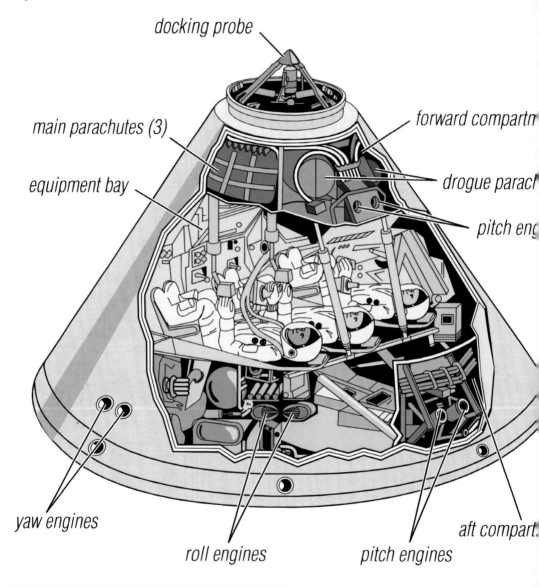

docking probe

main parachutes (3)

equipment bay

forward compartm

drogue parach

pitch eng

yaw engines

roll engines

pitch engines

aft compart.

The Apollo spacecraft Command Module was the control center and was designed for a three-astronaut crew. The module weighed more than 9,900 pounds (4,490 kilograms).

the moon's surface. The crew of *Apollo 13* never made it to the moon because of a damaged oxygen tank. The mission became known as a "successful failure" because, despite the accident, ground control worked tirelessly with the three astronauts and devised a successful plan to return them all safely to Earth. Project Apollo was completed in 1972 after the moon landing of *Apollo 17*.

After the Mercury, Gemini, and Apollo programs, the space race pressed on. There were even efforts to create

SKYLAB

Any difficult process includes successes as well as failures. Space exploration is no exception. Skylab was NASA's first attempt at a space station for research purposes. It was launched in 1973 and orbited 270 miles (435 kilometers) above Earth until 1979. Several crews of astronauts worked on Skylab in 1973 and 1974, researching many important concepts about spaceflight, including the effects of weightlessness on the human body over long periods of time.

After that success came a failure. The abandoned 165,000-pound (75,000-kilogram) space station broke up upon reentry to Earth's atmosphere in 1979. Much of the debris landed in the Indian Ocean and in Western Australia, which is largely undeveloped land. Fortunately, there were no injuries from the vehicle's dangerous crash to Earth. The crash emphasized the importance of strict and safe planning on every aspect of a spaceflight, from launch to landing.

a space station that would permanently stay in space for the purposes of research. That mission, launched in 1973, was called Skylab.

THE SPACE SHUTTLE

For thirty years, the space shuttle was NASA's reusable space transportation system. There were five space shuttle vehicles—*Columbia, Challenger, Discovery, Atlantis,* and *Endeavour.* A sixth shuttle, *Enterprise,* was built but never flown into space.

In 135 missions between 1981 and 2011, the shuttles were used to transport astronauts and cargo back and forth between Earth and space. Unlike previous space capsules that fell to Earth over the oceans, a space shuttle could fly back to Earth and land on a runway similar to an airplane.

Space shuttles were

The space shuttle *Discovery* is launched at Florida's Kennedy Space Center in 2006. At launch, the shuttle orbiter was powered by two booster rockets and an external fuel tank (*orange*). Soon after liftoff, the tank and booster rockets were discarded.

vertically, like other NASA rockets and space vehicles. The shuttle was attached to two booster rockets and a large orange fuel tank. The booster rockets propelled the shuttle into space. Once the rocket fuel burned for about two minutes, the boosters fell back to Earth and landed in the ocean so they could be reused in future missions. The shuttle also had its own rocket engines, which continued to fire for another six minutes. The large orange fuel tank detached and fell back to Earth, burning up in the atmosphere as it fell. Then the shuttle was in orbit. At the end of the mission, the shuttle landed similar to a glider.

Despite many successful missions, the shuttle program was marred by disasters. Two of the five shuttles, *Challenger* and *Columbia*, were lost in accidents that destroyed the crafts and killed the astronauts on board. Among those killed on the *Challenger* in 1986 was Christa McAuliffe, a high school teacher and the first civilian to go into space.

The last shuttle mission, flown by *Atlantis*, ended on July 21, 2011. After that, the remaining shuttles were moved to museums.

The crew members killed in the *Challenger* disaster of 1986 were (*back row, left to right*) Ellison Onizuka, Christa McAuliffe, Gregory Jarvis, and Judith Resnik; (*front row, left to right*) Michael Smith, Francis (Dick) Scobee, and Ronald McNair.

THE INTERNATIONAL SPACE STATION

The International Space Station (ISS) is a low-orbiting research station that is a cooperative effort of the United States, Russia, Japan, Canada, and the European Space Agency. Assembly of the ISS began with the launches of the Russian control module Zarya on November 20, 1998, and the US-built Unity connecting node the following month. These were linked in orbit by US space shuttle astronauts. In mid-2000, the Russian-built module Zvezda, a habitat and control center, was added, and on November 2 of that year the ISS received its first resident crew, comprising two Russians and an American, who flew up in a Soyuz spacecraft. A NASA microgravity laboratory called Destiny and other elements were later joined to the station, with the overall plan calling for the assembly, over a period of

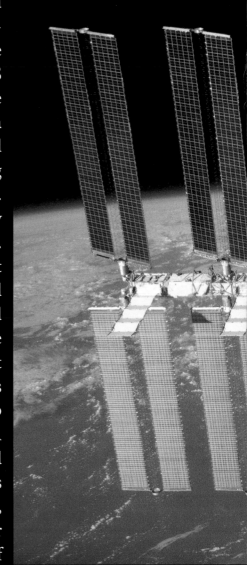

laboratories and habitats crossed by a long truss supporting four units that held large solar-power arrays and thermal radiators. Over the years, construction included the addition

Assembly of the ISS was begun in 1998 and completed in 2011. More than 115 spaceflights were required to assemble it. This 2011 photo of the ISS was taken by a crew member on the space shuttle *Endeavour*.

of a European-built American node, Harmony, which was placed on the end of Destiny. Harmony has a docking port for the space shuttle and connecting ports for a European laboratory, Columbus, and a Japanese laboratory, Kibo. The station has been fully operational since 2009 and can host a six-person crew.

Much of the research by ISS astronauts focuses on long-term life-sciences and material-sciences investigations in the weightless environment. Studies conducted by ISS crews and support staff back on Earth have led to a better understanding of the physical and psychological effects of long-term spaceflight on astronauts. ISS astronauts have also experimented with many different materials to see how well they can withstand the space environment. This work is crucial in preparations for future deep-space exploration, such as NASA's planned mission to Mars.

The space agencies that are partners in the ISS have not definitively decided when the program will end, but in 2010 the administration of US president Barack Obama announced that the ISS program would continue "likely beyond 2020." In 2014, the Obama administration indicated that the program would receive support until "at least 2024."

used to test if it was even possible to survive such a trip. In 1957, the Soviet Union became the first country to send an animal into orbit around Earth. It was a female dog named Laika. The dog survived the launch and weightlessness, which eventually paved the way for humans to go to space.

Laika, the dog that became the first living creature sent into space, is pictured onboard *Sputnik 2* in November 1957.

In 1961, the United States sent a five-and-a-half-year-old chimpanzee, Enos, into orbit aboard a Mercury spacecraft. Enos survived the mission. Spaceflight had no apparent effect upon the animals' ability to bear normal offspring.

During spaceflight, the human body is subjected to many stresses. Bone and muscle loss occurs in astronauts living in space for even a few days because of the virtual absence of gravity, a condition known as microgravity. Stresses and weight exerted on bones on Earth are signifi-cantly reduced in space. In these circumstances, calcium that has been stored in the bones is released into the bloodstream. This reduces bone density and puts astronauts at a higher risk of fracture upon their return to Earth. Extended missions have resulted in bone density loss of as much as 20 percent. The exact cause of bone loss is still unknown, but ongoing research hopes to slow or prevent the condition in astronauts for future long-term missions.

The virtual absence of gravity also affects blood flow. Blood that normally pools in the legs and feet shifts to the upper regions of a person's body. As a result, the face becomes

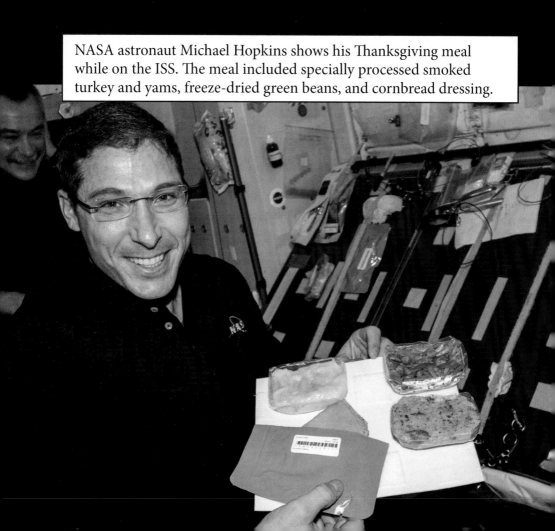

NASA astronaut Michael Hopkins shows his Thanksgiving meal while on the ISS. The meal included specially processed smoked turkey and yams, freeze-dried green beans, and cornbread dressing.

puffy and the person experiences headaches and sinus congestion. As the body attempts to compensate, the total blood production decreases. Upon returning to Earth, astronauts have been known to faint due to low blood pressure.

Food and nutrition in outer space require special consideration. Because spacecraft do not have refrigerators, food is stored in special containers to prevent spoiling. Packaging is also designed to help keep food particles from floating around and possibly damaging equipment. Some foods require hot or cold water to be added to them before they can be eaten. Many other foods are ready to eat, though they may require heating in the oven. The food given to astronauts is dense in nutrients to help them stay healthy and to combat the loss of bone and muscle mass that occurs during spaceflight.

Radiation is one of greatest dangers to astronauts. Exposure to high levels of radiation, including solar radiation, X-rays, gamma rays, and many other types, can harm living cells. Extended exposure may cause tumors and other serious health problems. On Earth, humans are protected from radiation by the planet's natural magnetic field. Almost all space missions have taken place close enough to Earth so that spacecraft were still protected by Earth's magnetic field. The Apollo moon missions, in which astronauts left the protection of Earth's magnetic field, were carefully timed to minimize the effects of solar radiation. Spacecraft and space suits have been designed to eliminate some forms of radiation, such as ultraviolet (UV) radiation.

NASA'S TWINS STUDY

Identical twin astronauts Scott and Mark Kelly took part in a study conducted by NASA to investigate the effects of spaceflight on the human body. Scott Kelly spent 340 days aboard the ISS and returned to Earth in March 2016. During that time, his brother, Mark, was back on Earth. Because of their identical genetic makeup and the fact that they are also both astronauts, NASA conducted a series of ten experiments to study differences between them that may have been caused by the space environment.

One experiment tested the Kellys' immune response to the flu vaccine in space as opposed to on Earth. Another experiment concentrated on the brothers' diets and the differences between the organisms in their digestive systems. According to NASA, "The Twins Study is a stepping stone towards long duration space exploration such as journeys to Mars." The results of this unique project are expected to be released in 2017 or 2018.

NASA astronaut Scott Kelly (*left*) and his identical twin brother, retired NASA astronaut Mark Kelly, talk to news reporters about the Twins Study in which they participated.

Astronauts cannot exit a spacecraft without the protection of a space suit. Space suits provide defense against extreme temperature changes and flying debris. They also store the oxygen and water that astronauts need to stay alive. A visor protects the astronaut's eyes from dangerous radiation.

On its website, NASA offers an interactive space suit to explain the suit's capabilities (https://www.nasa.gov/audience/foreducators/spacesuits/home/clickable_suit.html). It resembles a small spacecraft because it allows an astronaut to work outside a vehicle.

Getting into a space suit takes time because of the many layers of protection. Different parts cover the astronaut's head, chest, arms, hands, legs, and feet. No part of the body can be exposed to the elements. Water flows through tubes in the suit to keep the astronaut cool.

A backpack carries oxygen and removes the carbon dioxide that the astronaut breathes out. A fan circulates oxygen through the suit. The back of the suit also includes a device that has small thruster jets to help the astronaut return to the space station if he or she drifts too far off course during a space walk.

CHAPTER 3

BECOMING AN ASTRONAUT

The word "astronaut" comes from Greek words meaning "space sailor." The Russian space program uses the word "cosmonaut," which in Greek means "universe sailor." Both words reflect humankind's strong desire to learn more about what lies beyond Earth.

The men and women who have flown in space have been carefully selected and rigorously trained to withstand—and work efficiently in—the environment of space. The selection and training procedures for astronauts are similar in most countries.

REQUIREMENTS

Candidates for space travel must typically meet particular age and physical requirements. According to NASA, astronaut pilots in the US space program must be between 5 feet 2 inches (1.6 meters) tall and 6 feet 3 inches (1.9 m) tall. They must have a blood pressure of 140/90 and vision of 20/100 or better, which must be able to be corrected to 20/20. These physical requirements have been put in place because

NASA astronaut Scott Kelly trains inside a Soyuz simulator at the Gagarin Cosmonaut Training Center in Russia. Astronauts must undergo thorough preparation for each mission they undertake.

equipment is built to certain specifications and because the body must be able to endure the physical stresses of spaceflight. The requirements differ slightly depending on the particular job the astronaut performs in space.

In addition to the physical requirements for becoming an astronaut, there are also strict requirements in education and experience. To become an astronaut pilot, candidates need to have earned at least a bachelor's degree in math, engineering, or one of the biological or physical sciences, such as biology or physics. It helps if the candidate also has earned an advanced degree, such as a

As NASA commander Steve Swanson (*left*) supervises, flight engineer Reid Wiseman uses a tool during training for a space walk in the Partial Gravity Simulator test area at NASA's Johnson Space Center.

master's degree. A pilot candidate usually has extensive experience in flying high-performance aircraft and often has a military background.

Why do astronauts need such a technical background if the equipment they use is state-of-the-art and highly automated? For the astronauts' own safety, it is important to understand how the equipment works so they can make adjustments or repairs in case of emergency, such as a fuel leak. In addition, astronauts perform a lot of research in space, which requires knowledge of math, science, and

STAYING GROUNDED

Not all people who have careers with NASA are astronauts. Many jobs related to space exploration are performed by people who stay on the ground in mission control, research and development, and engineering. The list of people who never take off into space includes robotics specialists and computer scientists, who build and program unmanned vehicles that will be used in space. It includes aerospace engineers, who design, test, and redesign the latest spacecraft. It includes meteorologists, who make sure the weather conditions for takeoffs and landings are ideal. There are also many scientists working "on the ground" at NASA analyzing samples brought back from space missions and photos taken by unmanned vehicles and telescopes.

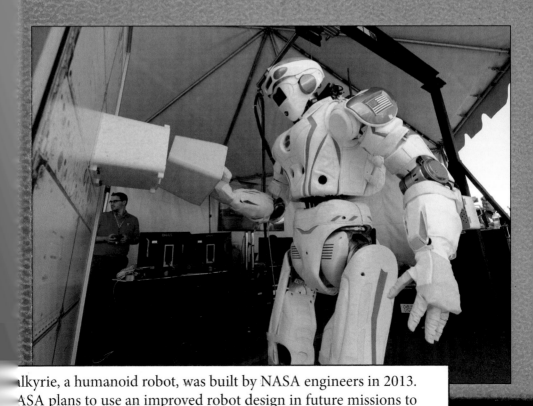

alkyrie, a humanoid robot, was built by NASA engineers in 2013. ASA plans to use an improved robot design in future missions to lp prepare habitats, such as on Mars, for humans.

motion, and energy are part of the job.

TRAINING

Once an applicant is accepted for training, the real work begins. The process of becoming an astronaut can take up to two years. Candidates gain detailed knowledge of the International Space Station and its systems. They receive flight training and learn how to perform extravehicular activity

A NASA astronaut participates in training for a space walk in the water of the Neutral Buoyancy Lab. Such practice helps astronauts prepare for work they will need to do outside their spacecraft.

(space walks). They study robotics and learn the Russian language so they can communicate with Russian mission control when necessary. Candidates also complete wilderness survival training and military water survival training.

Practicing for flight takes place in life-size mockups of space vehicles and the ISS. Astronauts learn how to move around the spacecraft safely and how to function in the nearly weightless conditions of space. One of the newest technologies uses virtual reality (VR) simulators that can mimic the visual environments that astronauts will encounter in space. For example, NASA's VR lab allows trainees to perform virtual space walks to help prepare them for the real thing.

Trainees also practice space walks by going underwater in a huge pool called the Neutral Buoyancy Lab. The underwater environment simulates the weightlessness that astronauts will experience during space walks.

CHAPTER 4

THE FUTURE OF HUMAN SPACEFLIGHT

Space exploration has been stimulated by a complex mixture of motivations. Alongside the desire for scientific knowledge, space research has been encouraged by competition between national governments as well as commercial profit. Underlying all space exploration, however, has been a vision of the outward movement of humans from Earth. Ultimately, these efforts might lead to permanent settlements in space.

LOOKING FORWARD

After the end of the space shuttle program in 2011, NASA designed the *Orion* spacecraft to replace it. *Orion* was designed to take astronauts farther into the solar system than they had ever traveled before. The first test flight of *Orion* was launched in December 2014.

NASA plans to launch future *Orion* flights on the new Space Launch System (SLS). This launch vehicle will be more powerful than any rocket that came before it. The SLS will be able to launch astronauts into deep space, including

An artist's concept shows an *Orion* spacecraft atop a powerful Space Launch System rocket. The system will eventually have a lift capability of 143 tons (130 metric tons) to propel missions into deep space.

asteroids and eventually Mars. The first mission to incorporate *Orion* and the SLS is scheduled to launch from the Kennedy Space Center in Florida in 2018. This unmanned flight will travel around the moon, farther into space than people have traveled before. The second planned mission will carry a crew.

MISSION TO MARS

Beginning in 2004, NASA landed a series of robotic vehicles called rovers on the surface of Mars. The rovers examined the surface to determine if Mars was, or is, capable of supporting life. This robotic exploration greatly increased knowledge of the Red Planet and helped preparations for manned missions to Mars. NASA has set a goal of sending humans to Mars by the 2030s. Finding a way for humans to sustain themselves

NASA's *Orion* spacecraft is designed to carry astronauts into space, offer emergency abort capability, support crew members during their space journey, and offer safe return to Earth from deep space.

in such a foreign environment is a challenge that NASA is investigating. The cost of the mission is a major factor to consider, as is the serious commitment that participants would have to make to such a mission.

The distance that humans have come in space travel in such a relatively brief time shows that we have much to look forward to in the near future. Pushing the boundaries of spaceflight will help scientists to discover more about

THE SOYUZ AND SHENZHOU PROGRAMS

After the US space shuttle program ended in 2011, Russia's Soyuz spacecraft was the only vehicle that could take astronauts to the ISS. First launched in 1967, Soyuz is the longest-serving manned-spacecraft design in use. In 2000 a Soyuz craft carried the first resident crew to the ISS. Since then at least one Soyuz has always been attached to the station in case an emergency forces the crew to return to Earth.

Other than Soyuz, China's Shenzhou is the only spacecraft that flies astronauts into space. The fifth Shenzhou flight carried the first Chinese astronaut into space in 2003. That made China the third country after Russia and the United States to launch a manned spacecraft. Later Shenzhou missions docked with the Chinese Tiangong space stations. The second station in the series, Tiangong 2, was launched in September 2016.

NASA's *Curiosity* rover took a "selfie" on Mars's surface. During its explorations, *Curiosity* has measured radiation levels and collected other data to help NASA scientists plan for a manned mission to Mars.

GLOSSARY

CARBON DIOXIDE Gas that people and animals breathe out during the process of respiration.

CONSTELLATION Group of stars forming a recognizable pattern in the sky.

EUROPEAN SPACE AGENCY A cooperative organization for space exploration consisting of twenty-two nations.

INTERNATIONAL SPACE STATION (ISS) Large space-craft that orbits Earth and is used as a research lab.

LUNAR Having to do with the moon.

MICROGRAVITY A condition of very weak gravity, which causes a sense of weightlessness.

Glossary

PREEMINENCE The state of being above others in rank.

RADIATION Energy that comes from a source in the form of waves or rays that cannot be seen.

SPACE LAUNCH SYSTEM (SLS) Launch vehicle designed by NASA to propel the next generation of US space vehicles after the space shuttle.

SPACE RACE Period of competition in space exploration between the Soviet Union and the United States.

SPACE SHUTTLE Reusable, rocket-launched US spacecraft that made 135 flights into space between 1981 and 2011.

SPACE WALK A period of activity by an astronaut outside a spacecraft in space.

SPUTNIK Any of ten artificial satellites launched by the Soviet Union. The launch of *Sputnik 1* in 1957 began the space age.

SUBORBITAL Involving less than a full orbit or revolution

FOR FURTHER READING

Angelo, Joseph A. *Human Spaceflight* (Frontiers in Space). New York, NY: Facts On File, 2007.

Eisele, Donn. *Apollo Pilot: The Memoir of Astronaut Donn Eisele* (Outward Odyssey: A People's History of Spaceflight). Lincoln, NE: University of Nebraska Press, 2017.

Friedman, Louis. *Human Spaceflight: From Mars to the Stars*. Tucson, AZ: University of Arizona Press, 2015.

Gibson, Karen Bush. *Women in Space: 23 Stories of First Flights, Scientific Missions, and Gravity-Breaking Adventures*. Chicago, IL: Chicago Review Press, 2014.

Gregersen, Erik, ed. *Manned Spaceflight* (Explorer's Guide to the Universe). New York, NY: Britannica Educational Publishing, 2010.

Houston, Rick, and Jerry Ross. *Wheels Stop: The Tragedies and Triumphs of the Space Shuttle Program, 1986–2011* (Outward Odyssey: A People's History of Spaceflight). Lincoln, NE: University of Nebraska Press, 2013.

Impey, Chris. *Beyond: Our Future in Space*. New York, NY: W. W. Norton & Company, 2015.

Jones, Tom. *Ask the Astronaut: A Galaxy of Astonishing Answers to Your Questions on Spaceflight*. Washington, DC: Smithsonian Books, 2016.

Mallick, Nita, ed. *Space Exploration* (The Study of Science). New York, NY: Britannica Educational Publishing, 2017.

Petranek, Stephen L. *How We'll Live on Mars*. London, UK: TED Books, Simon & Schuster, 2015.

Shayler, David J., and Ian Moule. *Women in Space: Following Valentina* (Springer-Praxis Books in Astronomy and Space Sciences). New York, NY: Springer, 2005.

Teitel, Amy Shira. *Breaking the Chains of Gravity: The Story of Spaceflight before NASA.* New York, NY: Bloomsbury Sigma, 2016.

White, Rowland. *Into the Black: The Extraordinary Untold Story of the First Flight of the Space Shuttle* Columbia *and the Astronauts Who Flew Her.* New York, NY: Touchstone, 2016.

WEBSITES

Because of the changing nature of internet links, Rosen Publishing has developed an online list of websites related to the subject of this book. This site is updated regularly. Please use this link to access the list:

http://www.rosenlinks.com/FETTS/spaceflight

INDEX

A

aerospace engineers, 33
Aldrin, Edwin E., 13
Apollo 1 tragedy, 13
Apollo 11, 13, 15
Apollo 13, 15
Apollo 17, 15
Apollo program, 6, 12–16, 26
Apollo-Soyuz Test Project, 6, 10
Armstrong, Neil, 6, 13
"astronaut," derivation of word, 30
astronaut requirements, 30–34
astronaut training, 34–35
Atlantis, 7, 16, 19

B

blood flow, effect of space-flight on, 25–26
bone density loss, 25

C

Canada, 20

Carpenter, Scott, 8
Challenger, 16, 18
China, 7, 40
Collins, Michael, 13
Columbia, 16, 18
Columbus (European lab, ISS), 22
Command and Service Modules (Apollo spacecraft), 13
computer scientists, 33
Cooper, Gordon, 8
"cosmonaut," derivation of word, 30

D

Destiny (microgravity lab, ISS), 20, 22
Discovery, 16

E

Eisenhower, Dwight D., 4
Endeavour, 16
Enos, 24,
Enterprise, 16
European Space Agency, 20